A Look in the Woods

By Jordan Avery

Dad took Lily to see Grandad.

At Grandad's house,
Lily pulled up her hood.

"Lily!" called Grandad.
"All set for a fun day?"

Lily just looked at him.

Grandad took Lily on a hike to a brook.

“I cooked snacks!” said Grandad.

Lily scoffed.

Lily pushed her hood back.

"Let's go and have a look in the woods," she said.

"There might be snakes
in the woods!" said Grandad.
"Let's stay put and read books!"

Lily stood.

"Please?" she said.

"As long as you stay close,"
said Grandad.

They pushed their way
into the bushes.

"Look!" called Lily.

Two chipmunks were in a chase at the foot of a tree.
One chipmunk had a good nut, and the other wanted it!

The chipmunks ran and ran.

Lily and Grandad shook
as they laughed.

“If we had stayed by the brook, we would have missed this!” said Lily.

They went back
and ate the snacks.

Lily felt full and happy!

CHECKING FOR MEANING

1. What does Grandad want to do in the woods? *(Literal)*
2. Why were the chipmunks chasing each other? *(Literal)*
3. Why do you think Lily pulled up her hood at the start of the story? *(Inferential)*

EXTENDING VOCABULARY

took	What is the base of the word *took*? Which words in the text rhyme with *took*?
brook	What is a brook? What is another word with a similar meaning that the author could have used instead of *brook*?
full	What does it feel like when you are full? What else can be full? What word means the opposite of *full*?

MOVING BEYOND THE TEXT

1. What is your favourite thing to do outside in nature?
2. What foods are good to take on a picnic?
3. Chipmunks are animals that live in North America. What do you know about chipmunks? What else would you like to know?
4. Grandad and Lily laughed so much they shook. Have you ever laughed that much? What happened? How did you feel?

TIME TO WRITE

Write about a time you saw something very funny.

PRACTICE WORDS

books
pulled
hood
look
good
cooked
pushed
bushes
took
brook
stood
foot
shook
looked
put
don’t
I’m
woods
full
you’ll
let’s